A Maximized Woman: Armed and Dangerous

Dr. Lorelle N. Rich

On Purpose Publications, Nashville, TN

A Maximized Woman: Armed and Dangerous

All rights reserved. No part of this book may be reproduced in any form without permission in writing from the author, except in the case of brief quotations embodied in church related publications, articles or reviews.

Published by
On Purpose Publications
Nashville, TN
www.onpurposepublications.com
Copyright © 2010

ISBN 9780982706114

Cover design by Vincent Alexander and PrecisionFX Graphics

Printed in the United States of America

Dedication

This book is dedicated to
the Holy Spirit,
my husband, Michael Rich Sr.,
my mother, Cynthia Strong, and
my Spiritual Father,
Bishop Joseph Warren Walker, III.

Thank you each for the ingredients. You have been instrumental in assisting my spiritual growth and discipline as God's Maximized Woman.

A Maximized Woman: Armed and Dangerous

Table of Contents

Introduction: Maximized with Power 1

EMBRACING NEW WHOLENESS 5

TAPPING INTO YOUR NEW SEASON 15

SEEK GOD'S PLAN FOR YOUR LIFE 29

ARMED FOR VICTORY 33

DEALING WITH YOUR WAITING SEASON 39

IT IS TIME TO TAP INTO YOUR POTENTIAL 49

NO LONGER IN THE DARK 53

BIRTHING FORTH THE WINNER WITHIN 59

ACTIVATE THE WARFARE MANUAL WITHIN 61

BIOGRAPHY OF THE AUTHOR 71

CONNECT TODAY WITH DR. RICH!! 72

A Maximized Woman: Armed and Dangerous

Introduction: Maximized with Power

 The steps of a woman are filled with interesting doors of opportunities, obstacles, and triumphant avenues of faith. As we embark upon this journey called life, we each are challenged to take risks that require faith and endurance. As we step forth to embark on these life-changing opportunities, we are forced to move past the limitations of our past and press toward the future of the unexpected, despite what challenges may surround us. I believe these elements assist in the formulation of a "Maximized" Woman.

Let's look at the definition of *maximize*. It means to reach one's full capacity. This leads me to ask you a few questions: What is your vision? What are your goals for the next three months? How are you going to move forth in these goals? These are the types of questions that I believe will be answered within as we take a journey to discover even greater dimensions of the greatness that is embedded within us as God's Maximized Women.

Allow me to clarify the concept of a maximized woman even more. A Maximized woman is one who is moving forward, armed with goals, and aspirations. She is one who has drive, purpose, and has made a determined decision to dive into the deep water, and not come up for air until she reaches her goal. This woman is dangerous to the enemy. You may still be pondering what makes this type of woman so dangerous?

1. She is on fire and filled with the God-given power to succeed with her FAITH.
2. She recognizes that her worth is not labeled by man but by God.
3. She takes hold of her future by standing on the Word of God and makes no apology for her beliefs.
4. She walks in a power-driven, Kingdom confidence which keeps her positioned to prosper.
5. The love of God landscapes her heart and

she is not intimidated by her emotions which attempt to persuade her heart to think differently.

Please let me make myself clear. A Maximized woman is not perfect and she has made some mistakes. Yet she refuses to allow the mistakes to hinder her from believing that she can **move forward!** Instead, she allows her mistakes to serve as stepping stones to reach higher levels of victory in her life. Therefore, I want every woman reading this book right now to stand up and say "That is me. I am God's Maximized Woman!"

Introduction

EMBRACING NEW WHOLENESS

 As we embark on this journey together, I am sitting in Pump It Up (a play center for kids). I have just finished jumping up and down on the inflatable balloons with my kids, releasing my stress, and reflecting on how the enemy works overtime to keep us from experiencing true freedom. The enemy has tried to damage or hinder women from tapping into *wholeness* since the beginning of time.

We must remember God created man (us) in His own image. We have to remember the Lord is not fragmented or divided. God is full and lacking nothing. God made man in His likeness and image, *whole.* Male and female created He, *them.* He called their name Adam (see **Genesis 5:1-2**). When God made Eve, He didn't reach down into the earth, into the foot, or finger of a man. He reached within a man. Therefore, Eve was created in the inner emotional and spiritual womb of man.

Thus, the relational parts of a woman are so unique and intrinsic that we ourselves cannot always fully understand. This is why the enemy works overtime to distort and bruise our inner emotions. This causes us to lift up walls and unhealthy barriers to survive the emotional roller coasters that come with friendships, with other sisters, and with people.

These distorted emotions cause us, at times, to desire acceptance and validation from sources that do not have the capacity to fulfill those needs. As we sort through these emotions, we open ourselves to levels of depression and oppression. This causes the warlike mentality to become weakened and we lose sight of the pursuit for wholeness.

The root cause of an unhealthy desire for acceptance is rejection. We must understand that, since the beginning of time, the enemy has worked overtime to create situations that left openings in our hearts. These openings have led us as women to be easy targets for unhealthy relationships and unhealthy decision making skills concerning our lives. We can no longer blame others for the bleeding that is still taking place in our hearts. Instead, we must apply God's love, begin to consciously renew our thinking, and begin to set new priorities.

    We also must seek wise counsel to assist us in moving forward. As we make steps to move forward, we must formulate target goals for our lives. This process should be targeted toward your spirit, mind, and body. Remember you are a three-fold, triune being, so all these areas must be examined to assist in the process of becoming whole within. You have been fragmented long enough. It is time for you to make it a Kingdom priority to initiate steps toward your goals to be WHOLE within!

    Please make a conscious to remember wholeness is God's plan for your life. God does not desire for you to make any apology for your depth to believe and confess His Word, despite what things look or feel like in the natural. So despite the hurts and disappointments that have occurred in your past with various friendships, especially sister-ships and career-ships, I want you to still have the desire to rise up in your God given confidence for **Hebrews 10:35** says, *"Do not throw away your confidence, which hath great recompense of reward."*

The word *confidence* in this scripture is the Greek word *paressia*, meaning boldness and depicts a very bold, frank, and outspoken type of language. It also carries the meaning of being forthright, blunt, direct, and straight to the point. In this verse, it refers to the bold, brave, and fearless declarations and faith confessions regarding God's promises that these believers had been professing.

In other words, the Hebrew Christians had been declaring and laying claim to the promises of God's Word in their lives. However, results were not birthing forth and they were becoming weary, feeling tempted to give up, and toss it all away. This verse urged them to keep believing and hold on tight to God's Word for their lives.

You must choose to move forward in the Word of God despite what your fickle emotions or tainted thoughts. This is your day to maximize your faith and trust in God's ability to bring your destiny to pass! You will not allow the fear of failure to slow down your momentum to move forward.

I decree the anointing and gifts that God has engrafted within your Spirit and urge you to stay focused. Do not allow the enemy to talk you into tossing away your faith. You have made it too far to walk away from God's promises at this time in your life!

I want us to study **Hebrew 10:35,** because there is a key element in this text on which we should meditate more extensively. **Hebrews 10:35** says, *"Cast not away…"* The words *cast not away* are taken from the Greek word *apoballo,* which is a compound of the words *apo* and *balla.* The word *apo* means *away.* The word *ballo* means *to throw something such as a ball or some other object.* When you compound these two words, the new word means to *throw away; to discard; to get rid of something no longer desired, needed, or wanted.*

Now, woman of God, I believe a Kingdom key to unlocking new dimensions of steady confidence in your life is to apply *apobolla* meaning *casting away*. Therefore, you have to make a decision to release and rid yourself of areas that are affecting and infecting your confidence to believe the Word of God.

Ridding yourself of these issues prevents you from casting away your ability to stand on the promises of God. An example of the word *apobolla* is found in **Mark 10:50.** Jesus had finished His ministry in the city of Jericho, and He and His disciples were to leave the city, along with a great number of people. As Jesus passed down the road, He walked right past a blind man named Bartimaeus.

Mark 10:47-48 says, *"And when he Bartimaeus heard that it was Jesus of Nazareth, he began to cry out and say, 'Jesus,* *thou son of David have mercy on me.' And many charged that he should hold his peace; but he cried the more a great deal, 'Thou son of David, have mercy on me.'"*

    You see, Bartimaeus' garment was so tightly wrapped about his body that it restricted him from getting to Jesus. Thus, the word *apobolla or casting away* is found in **Mark 10:50.** "And he casting away his garment, rose, and came to Jesus."

    In other words, Bartimaeus did not just remove his garment and lay it aside. Rather, he quickly jerked it off his body and threw it to the ground. He tore himself free of that garment which was restricting him from getting to Jesus.

    I am speaking to a woman right now still contemplating her destiny and her life. I want you to rise up and go forward in the power of God and tell yourself that this is not your season to stay stuck in a place of defeat and uncertainty. You have been empowered by God to press through and come forth victorious. So right now throw away those thoughts of doubt, abuse, and fear. Get rid of those old memories and tell some people and things in your life they have reached the EXPIRATION DATE! It is time for you to renew your life. The Word of God exclaims in **2 Corinthians 5:17,** *"Therefore, if anyone is in Christ he is a new creation; old things have passed away and all things are becoming NEW."*

While in the process of writing this book, I had to renew my driver's license because it had reached its expiration date. Due to my busy schedule, I had not made time to go to the driver's license renewal location. I thought the renewal process would be long, but also realized I was taking a chance driving with an expired license. Therefore, I made a decision to set aside the time to get my license. Once I made the decision, I immediately began to experience new liberty within. The amazing thing was once I arrive to the driver's location they had an *express lane* which gave me faster access to receiving my license. Now I know someone is catching this anointing. Because you never know when your obedience may elevate you to the EXPRESS LANE!!

Therefore, what you thought would take hours or months may be awaiting your arrival. The express lane was awaiting my arrival and the enemy was trying to paint illusions in my mind that it would take a long time absolutely interrupting my day. You know the enemy is a deceiver and he tries to plant seeds of concern in our minds to prohibit us from trusting God and moving forth in immediate obedience.

I DECREE right now to your mindset that you no longer have to wait in the back of the line. God is ready to accelerate you to the front, in order that you might be a walking testimony of God's ability to cause a Divine acceleration to move forth upon your life. Come on woman of God, catch this anointing...this is your NOW season!

14 | A Maximized Woman: Armed and Dangerous
Embracing New Wholeness

TAPPING INTO YOUR NEW SEASON

The Word of God exclaims in **Isaiah 43:19,** *"Behold I am doing a NEW thing and Now it springs forth, do you not perceive and know it will and will you not give heed to it?"* I believe this is a Divinely appointed word for the women of God. This is a NEW season for God to release His wind of favor upon His daughters. I know God has been stretching your faith and cleansing you from old impurities. Now you and others can recognize the true value of your worth, knowing the final outcome will be victorious because of who is on your team...Your Heavenly Father!

It is amazing how we can sense God challenging us to release some habits although we procrastinate in being obedient to His leading. Yet we want God to move expeditiously on our behalf when we have a request. As we prolong our decision to be obedient, we become *entangled* in bondage and restrict our ability to experience all that

God has awaiting us.

Thus, let's reflect on why the example of blind Bartimaeus, shared earlier, is so important to you. The actions of Bartimaeus symbolize your season to cast away mental and emotional restrictions that have been constantly causing you to doubt your ability to rise forth. Trust God's ability to work within you and activate new success, new peace, new joy and new ideas. As a maximized woman, it is your responsibility to shift the paradigm of your thinking concerning God's ability to perform His Word in your life. In **Hebrews 10:35,** God's response to you, *'that ye HOLD fast"* to your God-given FAITH!!

Come on women of God! This is our appointed season to take hold of God's promises for our lives and use our Kingdom authority to command the fullness of God's destiny to come forth. We will not allow the barriers of our past or present to prohibit us from moving forward. I want you to take a moment to reflect on things you are ready to *cast away* and then I want you to reflect on ways you are NOT going to cast away your Faith! Put the Word in action and push forth because the BEST is still yet to come in your life! If you believe what I am saying then give God a great "Hallelujah" shout with me!

I want you to pray this prayer:
Father God, I desire to be whole within; I desire whole friendships because I was created to be a WHOLE relational being. I push past the fear of rejection and decree; I am being re-generated within my mind, soul, and spirit, in Jesus name. I am maximizing the fullness of who You have created me to be since the beginning of time.

As you take time to really process what I've shared, I pray you are coming into a greater revelation of why the enemy has been so hard on your trail since you were a little girl. Even as I sit here on this child like bleacher, my own little-girl areas of how even in elementary school, the enemy worked overtime to stir up issues between me and my other little girl-friends. I think of how we would compete for who had the best ideas or who wore the best clothes. Then I think on how in junior high, I ran for high school queen and how, due to an intentional tampering with the votes, I lost. Then the girl who won actually asked my ex-boyfriend to be her escort. Even then, the stabbing wounds of rejection were beginning to formulate...nothing but the evil stabs of the ENEMY!

See, the enemy was recognizing the seed of potential within me and was working overtime to abort the healthy process of growth. So you might ask the question, "WHY does the enemy hate the woman so badly?" Well, remember God prophesied to the serpent that had seduced Eve into sin, that He was going to put enmity between the *seed of the woman* and *the serpent*. The word for *seed* in Hebrew is *zera,* which is also used as the word for *semen.* Women do not have semen but their womb is the birthing ground for the semen. And the descendent that was to be in the womb of Eve was the *man child* Jesus Christ.

As a result of God's prophecy, there is

ENMITY between you and the enemy. The definition of *enmity* is a state of ill will or hostility. The devil's target is to destroy your identity, your mind, your emotions, your husband, your children, your business, your church, your productivity, your health. He will do whatever it takes to achieve this in your life. The enemy is always looking for his next victim. In **1 Peter 5:8,** the Bible states, *"Be sober, be vigilant; because your adversary the devil, as a roaring lion, walketh about, seeking whom he may devour."* This scripture gives even more reason as to why you must REFUSE to remain in a victimized mentality, rise up with the *might* of God's anointing within, and choose to have a victorious mindset about your present condition. You might say, "I need assistance with this because I am ready for more consistent victory in my life."

Women of God, I believe that if we maximize our thinking by renewing it through the Word of God, we will develop more strategic ways of thinking in order to defeat and uncover the plans of the enemy against our lives. I believe a great strategy to use in your mental thinking to defeat the enemy is to think like an athlete, running a race. When a runner runs a race, they have one thing foremost in their mind—the FINISH LINE! It was with this thought that the Apostle Paul wrote the Corinthians, *"Know ye not that they which run this race all, but one will receiveth the prize? So run, that ye may obtain"* (see **2 Corinthians 9:24**).

The word *run* is the Greek word *trecho*, which depicts runners who run a foot race in a huge stadium before adoring fans. In order for the runner to run successfully and finish victoriously, the runner must commit his or her full strength and complete attention toward the goal. Paul had this in mind when he wrote this verse.

Thus, in order to run our race as God desires, it will mandate that we learn to run at a consistent pace. In other words, we cannot be in the race today and drop out tomorrow. We must stay in the race on a long-term basis so we can avoid losing our momentum and wearing ourselves out! You must make a decision woman of God, to stir forth the "finish-line anointing" within your mindset.

For example, Paul tells us that we are to run until we *obtain*. The word *obtain* in Greek is *katalambano,* which is "to fiercely seize or take hold of something." This portrays a runner who runs with might, using every last ounce of energy as he or she strains toward the finish line.

Likewise, if you want to grasp God's will for your life, there is no room for any attitude other than one of victory and boldness to continue to pursue your dreams, aspirations, ministry, and healing. But the key to achieving this repair is to keep your eye on the finish line!

Apostle Paul suffered hardship, lack, cold, homelessness, trouble, nakedness, lack in the city, wilderness, and the sea. Yet he never lost sight of the fact that he was called of God. Therefore, like Paul, you must not lose sight that you have been called of God for this appointed hour. You must have resolve, high morale, courage, strength, tenacity, persistence, and an unrelenting mindset. You must get up out of your old mindset and take your stand (see **2 Corinthians 10:5**).

Let me remind you, sitting around hoping for something to happen will not cause anything to birth forth in your life! You must take responsibility for your life and jump in the race with your sisters for Christ. Fix your eyes on the goal, put on your Kingdom racing shoes, and run with all your might to the finish line!

I am speaking to you woman of God. I want to remind you that it is your TIME. Therefore, choose this day to make the decision to step forth into the vision God has planted within you and go the distance! You can do it! I believe in YOU. I decree that your condition is changing and you are no longer a victim to the wiles of the enemy. You are choosing to tell failure, disappointment, and fear to loose you from within because you are taking BACK what the devil stole, in Jesus name!

To survive the assaults of the enemy, you must move into the right place with God by staying plugged into God's spirit. You must feed on the Word of God and allow the Word to be your power source. You must stay connected to God's love and allow His anointing to be your life source. Maximize the fullness of the ability to have life and to have it more abundantly (see **John 10:10**).

As you triumphantly EXHALE and release yourself from your past, you must now teach yourself to daily inhale your true identity. I just finished shooting some basketball hoops with my son at Pump It Up. Each time I dunked the ball, I would say "HUUH!" visualizing myself dunking on the head of the enemy. Now to hit the rim of the goal, I had to jump really hard and I had to take a breath in. But once I released the ball, I would EXHALE! Come on maximized woman, stand on your feet and *bruise* the head of the enemy with your new recognition of identity!

In **Romans 16:20**, Paul writes, *"The God of peace shall bruise Satan under your feet shortly...."* The word *bruise* is taken from the Greek word *suntribo*, a word that actually means the notion of trampling the devil under your feet. The word historically denoted the act of smashing grapes into wine. However, it also referred to snapping, breaking, or crushing bones.

Now, if you noticed in this verse, Paul uses the word *shortly*. This word actually comes from a military term describing the formation of Roman soldiers. They were instructed by their commanders, "You are Roman soldiers! Lift up your feet high, stomp loud, and let everyone know you are enroute into town. And if someone is foolish, to stand in your way—do not stop to ask them to move! Just keep marching, stomping, and pounding! Now that is walking in Kingdom authority.

So when Paul uses the word *shortly,* he is referring to stomping or crushing steps. Now please remember, Roman soldiers wore shoes that were spiked with nails on the bottom. These shoes were described as killer shoes because they were not normal (see **Ephesians 6:14-15**). This should remind you of those *high, pencil-thin heel shoes we women wear sometime* (smile). Thus, use your heel to trample on the head of the enemy and not each other.

Women of God, it is time for us to rise up as a mighty army. Put on your ARMY HEELS to trample on the head of the enemy when he TRIES to get in the way of our destiny. Do not ask him to move politely, but with Holy FIRE! If the enemy is dumb enough to challenge and try to prohibit God's plans from coming forth in your life, then according to this verse, God tells you to *just keep walking and raise your feet high, smash down as hard as you can, and bruise him beyond recognition with the HEELS of your feet!*

Come on join me right now! Go to your closet, put on the highest heels you have, and begin to walk around with authority in God knowing you are destroying the enemy. All the ladies with heels shout "YES!!!"

However, it is important that I point out that this smashing and crushing of Satan must be done in cooperation with God. Please let me remind you that alone you are no match for your archenemy. This is why in **Romans 16:20**, Paul says *"The God of peace shall bruise Satan under your feet...."* In other words, this is a joint partnership of you and God. And with God as your partner, you shall be victorious!

Come on women of God! Let's take back everything the enemy has stolen. Your God ordained mission is to reinforce the victory of Christ Jesus, which is already won and demonstrate how terribly defeated Satan already is! Therefore, your healing, financial blessings, and your miracle already belongs to YOU!

Your identity is in Christ Jesus. He accomplished a complete, total, perfect work through the Cross of Calvary and His resurrection from the dead (see **Romans**

6:17). So, maximize your new identity in Christ and partner with God, in order for His glory to be manifested in the earth realm for all to see that Jesus Christ is LORD!

SEEK GOD'S PLAN FOR YOUR LIFE

As a maximized woman, armed and dangerous, you must not allow the limited external material things of life to dress your identity. Don't allow things like the Mercedes, money, nails, and hair—real or fake (smile)—to be the source of your identity. Remember, all these things are temporary and can dissolve at any moment.

Until you recognize that God is the ONE who has given you life—the One who designed and fashioned you with a specific plan and destiny in mind—you will continue to walk in confusion and seek the wrong avenues to find purpose. It is time that we stop allowing other people to breathe their dreams and plans into our hearts without first discovering the plans God has for our lives (see **Jeremiah 29:11**).

We need to seek the face and heart of God for our true identity. When God blew from His own breath into our being, we became alive. **Job 33:4** says, *"The spirit of God has given me, and the breath of the Almighty has given me life."* There are many women who wake up every day *just making it*, just beating the air. This type of woman is really without purpose, without direction, or impact.

Yet a transformation is occurring and God's Word is birthing forth newness within you spiritually and psychologically. Therefore, you are beginning to visualize yourself no longer ordinary, but extraordinary, despite the trials and tribulations you have encountered.

Now you are changing the wardrobe of your thoughts about life and being properly prepared for the new place of confidence that you are seizing hold of. Thus, your faith is causing the anointing of God to uproot areas of procrastination, fear, doubt, and uncertainty.

As a woman of new definition, you are no longer being defined by your natural achievements. Instead, you are now riding on cruise control and allowing the hand of God to drive your destiny, causing new Kingdom paradigm shifts to take place in the reshaping of your thinking. Yes, God's woman of Destiny, you are now plugging into real Kingdom Victory with lasting results!

ARMED FOR VICTORY

The reshaping of your Kingdom thinking prohibits you from settling for second best which is a key ingredient to maximizing the fullness of your Destiny. You are no longer stagnated by the fears of life because you are becoming armed and dangerous within your inner man. God has innovatively created you to have potent power that is targeted to destroy the enemy.

The danger of you as a maximized woman is the alertness in your Spirit that can spot danger before if comes forth. See, you bruise the enemy by just having the ability to recognize his subtle plans before they even manifest. A maximize woman has a prayer zone, in other words, when she taps into the Spirit realm, the momentum of victory begins to rise within that causes things to turn around for her family, her community, and for her personal self. Choose to step forth into new arenas of victory because you are ready for a new start.

Each of us has been designed by God to carry measures of greatness. These measures of greatness are subjected to various life disappointments that can interrupt the growth pattern of healthy success.

Yet, we still have the ability to reach forth and tap into God's greatness within us if we choose to tell our emotions and feelings to be quiet and to *"walk by faith and not be sight"* (see **2Corinthians 5:7).** We have to choose to speak life instead of death. Remember *"faith is something that is hoped for, the evidence of things not seen"* (see **Hebrews 11:1**).

The feelings within you may say, "I am afraid, this might not work." Even though you may feel afraid, you have to still walk by faith! One of the key elements to becoming a maximized woman is to make a choice. You must choose to push forth and choose to make it. You must choose to believe that His burden is light and His way is easy (see **Matthew 11:30**).

You have to choose to move forth and take Kingdom authority over excuses. Excuses stagnate in your ability to move forward. Thus, you have to choose faith over problems, sickness, circumstances, and doubt. I will say it again, it is a choice. As women of God, we must stand and employ our Kingdom tenacity. We must aggressively take hold of our future despite the difficulties that surround us. We must realize the Kingdom inheritance that has been designed for our lives by our Heavenly Father.

The power recognizing the Kingdom understanding within allows us to use our faith and decree the Word of God with confidence and trust. This type of faith recognition is a way to maximize the greatness within yourself by refusing to give room or provision to your feelings. **Romans 13:14** says that we should make no *provision* for the flesh or the enemy. Making provision means *to supply, to make due preparations, to arrange, cater, plan, fix up with*. Thus, we should keep our flesh under subjection to the Spirit. We must take time to read the Word, pray, and fast in order to condition our flesh to learn how to submit to the will of God. Oh, I know how our emotions try to override our faith. That is why we are to *"resist the enemy"* (see **James 4:7**).

When the enemy comes knocking at your door with thoughts of discouragement, anxiety, jealousy, coveting, fear, torment, lust, etc., stop opening the door of your mind by saying, "Come on in, you are right." Instead, say "NO, I refuse to make room for you; I have the victory and command you to leave NOW in Jesus name!"

Come on MAXIMIZED woman! Use your Kingdom authority and take a stand within your thought patterns. Remember, you have greatness within you. And today, you choose to no longer be defeated by the limitations of life because the redeeming blood of Christ Jesus has purchased you.

Remember, you have a new DNA clothed in royalty which has been engrafted in your bloodline. You are choosing to not allow the illusions of the enemy to speak lies to you because God's truth is your portion (see **1 Peter 2:9**).

During difficult times of testing and trials, we must choose to rise to the occasion and understand we our being put to the test. Therefore, when the enemy comes in like a flood (see **Isaiah 59:19**), we must rise up, take hold of the might or power of God within, and choose to draw closer to Him. You must remember when the enemy begins to sense the greatness in our lives is rising forth to a new place of victory, he begins to heighten the FIRE of the warfare.

You must remember that the enemy is not all knowing, but that he monitors when you are focusing, developing a consistent prayer life, and gaining new revelation of the Word of God. Therefore, the enemy begins to try to birth forth intimidation to cause you to lose confidence in your ability to finish the race. Even now, I want to stop to encourage someone who feels tired or worn out, to RISE forth and I decree a fresh anointing to pour forth upon you NOW in Jesus name!

DEALING WITH YOUR WAITING SEASON

 As women of God, we are tested by seasons of *waiting*. And the reality is, many of us do not prefer to wait on God. As I reflect on seasons in my ministry, there were times I knew God was stirring me to step forth and trust Him. However, in various projects the final results seem to linger. Even though I would cry to God, I would faithfully hear Him consistently say "Wait on my timing."

Even in the midst of writing this book, I just finished having a conference with my Spiritual father Bishop Joseph Walker, III of the Mount Zion Baptist Church. Interestingly, I know my meeting with him was a God appointment because his schedule is usually over booked.

In our meeting, I asked guidance about my destiny. And like any Spiritual father who knows their spiritual daughter, he said "You know Lorelle, you have always had to work on not being too impatient." I smiled as if to say, "You are correct." Then he instructed me to refocus, stop pursuing the dream, and let it pursue me. In other words, he was in no way telling me to take a seat and do nothing, but to realign my heart and its true intent in ministry.

Now to assist in this refocus you must position your Spirit to *delight* in the Lord. The Word says in **Psalm 37:4**, *"Delight yourself also in the Lord and He will give you the desires and secret petitions of your heart."* The word *delight* means "a high degree of pleasure or satisfaction." Whenever you find yourself in a struggle, you must learn how to *delight*. You must learn that when God give orders, you cannot have it your way.

The will of God will not always be comfortable or understandable. Yet, you can paralyze the enemy by delighting in the Lord! The enemy is trying to trip you because God is moving you up from where you are now. As God's maximized woman, you must know God's purpose in your life shall come to pass.

Come on. Take a few minutes right there in that bedroom, office, or car and just ask the Holy Spirit to assist you in stirring forth a high degree of pleasure in your Heavenly Father and His plans for your life.

Every God-fearing woman should realign her heart's one true intent. It is something you personally do with God in your quiet time and then you allow patience to become your portion. The Word says in **Hebrews 10:36**, *"Patient endurance is what you need now, so you will continue to do God's Will. Then you will receive all that he has promised."*

Now as maximized women, we should know that patient endurance in waiting is not natural waiting. To *wait* on God means to stand in the faith of expectation of His appointed time. Therefore, this does not mean to curl up on the couch and do nothing. Instead, you are to activate your faith (start writing that book, order those business cards, write down target dates for those bills to be paid) and continually move forward in doing the natural things necessary for the fulfillment of the promise.

In other words, you should constantly monitor whether you are remaining in God's Divine will. It is so easy to get off course and lose sight of the true goal which is to ultimately have a heart of passion for the pursuit of God and His perfect will. See, now you are illustrating God's definition of *WAITING*.

One thing I am grateful for is having a purpose driven mother (thanks mom) who displayed to me what it meant to follow your dreams and never settle for less. Her example of courage has enabled me to rise up despite the disappointments and overwhelming pressures of life.

I remember how she would always speak words of life and give nuggets of wisdom on how to never settle for less than God's best for my life. Even despite the sometimes heated disagreements on various areas of my life, she would never let me start something and not complete it. I bless God for this because these types of ingredients have assisted in the growth of my ability to stay tenacious in God's plans for my life.

Now you might be saying, "I did not have that type of example." Well, I believe that is the purpose for which God has allowed our paths to cross. In the first chapter of the Book of Ruth, Ruth had a divine interruption when her path crossed to meet Naomi. In the story, Ruth married Naomi's son. When the son died, Ruth still chose to follow the God that Naomi served.

The beauty of this divine interruption was that Naomi caused the ingredients of Ruth to move past her fear and step forth into a new experience of faith. What were some of the steps that caused Ruth to experience effective results?
- She followed the instructions of Naomi when she was directed to glean in the field of Boaz (see **Ruth 2**).
- She chose to glean from the field with a heart that was knitted to ensure the care of Naomi was a top priority (see **Ruth 2:18**).

- She allowed herself to follow the instruction of Naomi who directed her to change her outward look. Maybe it is time for you to dress neater, find clothes to compliment your figure, and ensure applying a little make up to flow with your complexion (see **Ruth 3:3**).
- Ruth also applied wisdom in listening to the direction of Naomi who told her to lie at the feet of Boaz. Se could have chosen to take a different route, but her heart of humility allowed stability to occur in her life (see **Ruth 3:4-5**).

As you read these applications, are there areas that you need to apply with more effectiveness? If so, I believe you are reading this book because you have met your NAOMI (Prophetess Rich). Therefore, to activate this Divine connection, stop right now and email me at lsrtalks@aol.com. Let the enemy know by faith and activate your faith connection right now!!

The power of our lives coming together is not by coincidence but Divine Providence! I believe as our faith touches and agrees, things in your life will begin to take new steps of hope and stability. Come on maximized woman! Let's link arms, and become even more Armed and Dangerous!

The life of Ruth is an illustration of how we as maximized women must grow consistently the rate that God has designed for our lives. I believe we each have a designed *"SET TIME of favor"* (see **Psalm 102:13**). This set time is called *Kairos timing*. This occurs when God aligns things in your life with His omnipotent hand and supernaturally puts things into Kingdom motion.

This activation process usually comes after a season that seems to be dormant. In nature, there are seasons called *dormant* times, but please do not confuse this with meaning you are a *doormat*. During this dormant time, it appears that things are not thriving, growing, or flourishing. But this is not true because in reality, growth is really taking place.

This process occurs in our lives when we go through times of difficulty that cause us to experience pain, stress, depression, hurt, and fear. Yet, we may not recognize that these uncomfortable experiences are really causing deeper rooted levels of growth in preparation for your Divine appointed DUE season.

See, the roots on a plant have to grow downward before you view the final outcome of the flower. The stronger the roots are in a flower, the more stability it has to maintain longevity during the various weather conditions. This allows a plant to have conditioning power to weather a storm and not be blown away by the climate changes that come with life.

This same type of sustaining power is what God wants in our lives (see **Psalm 1:3**). I want to encourage you, do not be afraid of the processing stages. You have to be willing to press through with determination and courage. I truly understand how God's timing can seem to be so eternal and when you are ready to give birth, it seems as though God has forgotten you. But you are not forgotten.

You are God's special rose. So continue to water yourself like a plant with the water of God's Word for God *"watches over His Word to perform it"* (see **Jeremiah 1:12**).

Continue to water your life by stirring forth praise and worship in your mouth and *"bless the Lord at all times...His praise shall continue to be in my mouth"* (see **Psalm 34:1**). You must imagine yourself blossoming forth despite the climatic conditions of life. Remember every situation is temporary and can change at any moment. Do you believe that God would make the investment of giving His *"Only Begotten Son"* for you to live (see **John 3:16**) and then *not* allow you to birth your dreams or aspirations?!

The devil is a LIAR and this time you will not be seduced to believe the lies of the enemy because you are rooted in God's Truth! Get off that couch, turn that television off, and begin to shout forth your victory. Stand on your feet. Walk around that house. Command the enemy to give back everything he stole, with interest, in Jesus name!

I decree prophetically, that God is not finished with you. His name is written upon your life by the blood of Jesus and this is your set time! Now choose to tell your mind to believe and conceive the promises of God NOW!!

IT IS TIME TO TAP INTO YOUR POTENTIAL

The reality of a maximized woman is that she can conceive her potential. It amazes me how easily we, as God's maximized women, so easily succumb to the tactics of the enemy concerning the talents embedded within us. We hold back on dreams and love due to the inability to push past the thoughts of inferiority or fear of rejection. We begin to revisit the memories of the past and allow the identity of our nature to be molded by these clouded images. We fight with secret voices that constantly remind us of what we have not accomplished and seem to always overlook the steps we have achieved.

We maintain walls of defense as if we constantly need to prove something to people who could really care less about our present or our future. These loose ends keep us entangled by unhealed areas within our souls causing all kinds of sickness, overworked organs like kidneys, and stomach problems. Not to mention the stress that causes high blood pressure and diabetes. These unhealed areas become places of vulnerability to which spirits attach themselves. In counteracting these demonic strongholds, we must apply the blood of Jesus and repent in order to replace what has been stolen by the enemy. Wrestling in the spirit realm prolongs the process, yet we must stand in the assurance that we are *"redeemed from the curse of the law"* (see **Galatians 3:13**).

    The redemption of your new nature requires a daily vitamin of faith to ensure results. Your faith is the victory that conquers the world (sickness, poverty, bondage, and pressure) (see **1 John 5:4**). As you plug into the fullness of the substance of your Kingdom DNA, you will have a renewed perspective on who is fighting on your behalf; the Lord who is strong and mighty in battle (see **Psalm 24**). *Might* is the anointing for the battle. This *might* is working on your behalf within your new bloodline.

Let me explain this anointing to you. It causes burdens and yokes to be removed (see **Isaiah 10:27**). Therefore, *might* is the power to get the job done. Thus, this part of the DNA that lives within you causes you to walk in new empowerment, to turn on the switch of new understanding, and to participate and experience the fullness of God's best for your life!

I want to bring to your attention another form of *power* that allows you to walk victoriously. That is, the *Ischuous* Power of God. In **Ephesians 6:10** the Word says, *"Finally brethren, be strong in the Lord, and in the power of his might."* The word *might* in this verse is the word *ischuous*. It conveys the picture of a very, very strong bodybuilder or a mighty man with great muscular capabilities. Paul pictures God as ONE who is able, mighty, and muscular working on your behalf behind the scenes.

Therefore, the next time you run into a situation that seems a bit extreme, remind yourself that *"Greater is he that is in you than he that is in the world"* (see **1 John 4:4**). You have no need to allow fear or timidity to overcome you. There is enough power at work within you to resist any tactic that comes against you and to supernaturally remedy any circumstance that requires a change!

Let me decree to you woman of God that this *ischuous* power is now energizing the *kratos* power (the demonstrated, outwardly manifested, eruptive power of God) which is also in **1 John 4:4**. Thus, you are ready to heal the sick, raise the dead, cast out devils, pray with power and authority, speak words of faith, and see mountains move instantly! You better tap into the POWER that resides within you and refuse to be powerless! Maximize your POWER!

NO LONGER IN THE DARK

 The enemy is a great deceiver and he loves to bring messages of defeat and confusion. This is why the bible says to take every thought captive and make it obedient to Christ (see **2 Corinthians 10:5**).

Now, as we turn to the aspect of warfare that attacks the power of a woman, one of the first hurdles you must overcome is the battle of the mind. The greatest milestone in our journey as we walk forth in victory is when we are able to stay alert and on watch to what thoughts are downloading from the Spirit realm into our thinking.

The strategies of the enemy are to hijack our thinking and cause us to become unaware of what we are truly dealing with. We must take hold of the boldness of Christ within and be determined to no longer be left in the dark but instead bring our thoughts to the marvelous light. We must shine the light of God's Word on these thoughts, press forth beyond little-girl fears, wounded emotions, and trust God to restore and repair the areas that plague our lives.

One of the areas that is a very important weapon in the arsenal of a woman is her conscience. The conscience is the window between the soul and spirit. The conscience stores the memory patterns of your life. Our lives have been filled with various incidents and traumas that have left bruises and deep cuts. Unfortunately, some of these areas were covered up with natural band-aids in hopes that the bleeding would stop. Yet, despite the band-aids, the sensitivity of these unhealed places has still lingered in the conscience of our lives and caused a clouded perspective on our views of life and God.

This clouded view also affects one's ability to move forward. Our conscience is the key to us truly seeing! You have to see victory within to obtain it. You have to see wealth upon your life to obtain it. These are just a few examples of the power of seeing.

If you are blinded to the ability to see ahead, you cannot move ahead. And the conscience is a key element that speaks to secret places of your heart causing you to turn away from what you really have the God ability to achieve. In **Genesis 3:7**, when Adam and Eve sinned, their eyes *were opened*. Their lower nature was opened and they could no longer see from a heavenly viewpoint. They were now subject to using their natural senses, instead of their Kingdom faith.

Subjection to the natural senses paralyzed them from being able to maximize the fullness of their Kingdom ability. What has paralyzed you? Or what is inhibiting you from moving forward into the next step of your victory? You have the ability to still proceed forth despite the barriers you have encountered. You can overcome these areas by allowing the healing of your conscience to be a priority in your life.

These are a few steps to obtaining a healed conscience through the power of the blood:

1. **You must recognize the purification of the blood of Jesus.** You have to confess daily that your conscience be purified in the blood of Jesus. Remember, for something to be *purified* means it is cleansed or washed to be renewed. Trust by faith that the blood of Jesus has supernatural power to cleanse you of your past, no matter how deep it is. See, when the window of your conscience is cleansed through the confession of your sin, which is forgiven through the blood of Jesus (see **Hebrews 9:11-15**).

2. **You must know that God has sanctified you.** In other words, trust in the forgiving supernatural power of the blood of Jesus. In your own strength, you do not have the natural ability to release some issues or people. But believe that the power of the blood by faith is inwardly disconnecting you from those deep hurts causing those wounded areas to dissolve and lose their ability to speak to your life. You will no longer be

moved by the images that try to come up in your thoughts and speak to your heart because the blood of Jesus has washed YOU! (see **Hebrews 9:20-25**)

3. **You must believe you are regaining your sight to SEE again.** The blood of Jesus is now causing a fresh, new imprint of understanding to engraft your thinking, causing your thoughts to be reprogrammed (see **2 Kings 6:17- 20**).

    You cannot allow the power of unbelief and uncertainty to push you into the old, bitter, and familiar patterns of thinking. This is a new season for you and the power of God within you has the ability to arrest any obstacles that try to hinder you from moving forward. You are a woman that has survived many storms; therefore you shall come forth with greater levels of stamina and perseverance in this new season of your life if you choose too. Again, if YOU choose to!

BIRTHING FORTH THE WINNER WITHIN

A winning attitude is the motivation of a maximized woman, Armed and Dangerous. She not only wisely discerns that the various aspects and experiences of her life equate to the person she has become, but makes allowances for those equations to evolve further by positively interpreting them through the lens of hope, faith, and joy. The warring thoughts of defeat are pulled down into the obedience to God's word.

The winning attitude of God's maximized woman is one that is continuously taking a stand and having a heart of pursuit. To pursue one's destiny means to reach forth and recover all that the enemy has stolen. As a result, this woman is not satisfied with mediocrity. She understands God has called her to deeper dimensions and is prepared to take the dive. So many times we allow our physical condition to have dominion over the circumstance.

We must be determined to deal with the obstacles of life and not allow ourselves to become *weary* with pursuing our dreams. We combat the wiles of the enemy by reminding ourselves that *"these signs shall follow them that believe; In my name shall they cast out devils; they shall speak in new tongues; they shall take up serpents; if they drink any deadly thing, it shall not hurt them; they shall lay hands on the sick and they shall recover* (see **Mark 16:17-18**).

I prophesy to you to rise and move out of the place of defeat. Take hold of the fullness of your victory in Jesus name! You are an overcomer by the blood of the Lamb! Now begin to imagine yourself dressed in a new suit called LIFE and refuse to imagine sickness, fear, or doubt. You are God's WINNER! So LIVE, Woman of God! LIVE. *"He came to give you life and it more abundantly"* (see **John 10:10**).

ACTIVATE THE WARFARE MANUAL WITHIN

The warfare manual is within you as a woman. It takes maturity to activate it because you were designed to use proper artillery. Many times women make mental decisions to sign up for the warfare, but never show up to fully activate their position. In this season, you must decide not to make childish decisions. You must evaluate the cost before making the commitment.

A very important element that must be activated within a woman of maturity is the restoration of her inner conscience to swallow the pill called commitment. In other words, as a woman of God healed within, you are no longer vulnerable to making quick, rash decisions that are not based on substance. The formula to this process requires taking various healing steps.

Let's begin these steps.

Step 1:
Implant God's Word

- Become a student of the Bible. *"You must measure and study the thought you give to the truth which will be the measure that comes back to you"* (see **Mark 4:24**).
- When you have to deal with a situation, apply the Word of God immediately.
- Take time to understand your thoughts and examine where you are mentally based on the Word of God. Remember, God's Word is a lamp (see **Proverbs 6:23**).

Implementing these steps of faith and determination will assist in disciplining your thoughts and cause you to walk in new levels of success in your walk with God.

Step 2:
Move from the old self consciousness to the new God consciousness

Another area in the warfare manual that you must be willing to apply after the IMPLANTATION of God's Word is the need to rid yourself of thinking according to the world's standard.

- You must think according to God's standards and not the norms of the world.
- You must begin to think as God thinks, despite the circumstances.
- You must learn to recognize thoughts that contradict God's Word and His standards.
- You must separate yourself, from yourself and from your unregenerate thoughts (see **Ephesians 4:21-24**).

Are you applying the steps? Because the warfare mantle upon you as God's maximized woman is getting prepared for the battle. Your steps are causing things within your conscience to remain in Kingdom alignment.

Step 3: Pursue without distraction

The manual has another process that requires your attention.

- Refuse to dwell on things you see (circumstances). They are temporary and subject to change (see **2 Corinthians 4:18**).
- Study the enemy's tactics and stay alert to his weapon called distraction.
- Distraction is an intrusion of the mind that causes confusion.
- Keep in mind. Focus is necessary, for God brings peace not confusion.
- Stay alert! If Satan can distract you from your focus (the Word of God), he wins.

THE WAR IS ON!

 Women of God! There is a spiritual battle going on. And every woman of God is called to be a soldier in God's army. Now, because you have studied your manual, you have mentally come to the understanding of the importance of being prepared for war. Being unprepared can be detrimental—which is why you are prepared!

You are prepared because you are equipped through the Word of God to be victorious in every battle that you have to deal with in life. You are no longer the underdog that is victimized by the enemy. Instead, you have found that the battle has already been won because the devil is a defeated foe. Jesus defeated him thousands of years ago.

Because the enemy has been bruised through the years by the foot of women, he wants us so badly to be seduced into believing that on a personal level we are defeated. Yet the champion within us is rising forth and now we shall *"endure hardness as a good soldier"* (see **2 Timothy 2:3**). One thing is for sure, hard times help you to uncover what is really within you. We are building new forces of faith and courage within by reminding ourselves, we are God's soldiers built to stand against the powers of darkness.

Now let's take a minute to examine what a soldier is called to do in a battle. A soldier is called to walk in strength and to fight against the enemy. So as women of God, we are allowing the Word of God to feed the muscle of our faith and we are refusing to eat on junk food like the cares of the world. As God's soldiers, we have to remember; we have great influence that comes through the authority of Jesus Christ who is our Lord and Savior and we know at the name of Jesus demons must Flee!

A soldier understands orders (of attack, retreat, or block) and the importance of obedience. The understanding of order allows God's woman to walk in wisdom as a wife or a servant for the Kingdom of God. She is careful with her response to authority because of the importance of submission. She allows her actions to be reflected in the love and kindness of God. This type of obedience causes the hand of God to supernaturally cover her steps as she presses forth to WIN THE BATTLE!

The empowerment of walking in the maximized victory for the Kingdom must be activated with urgency. The importance of staying alert when on duty requires you to be armed with the proper artillery. The spiritual battles are clearly not with flesh and blood, (contending with physical opponents only), but against spiritual forces of wickedness in the unseen realm (see **Ephesians 6**).

Now with the battle plans within your Spirit, you are more alert and discerning of what strategy to take. So maybe the enemy is trying to seduce you and make you think, "I will be broke" or "no one cares for me" or "I am not needed." But now you are PREPARED to take ACTION! You are now tightening the belt of truth, putting on the breastplate of righteousness, lifting up the shield of faith, taking the helmet of salvation and the sword of the Spirit which is the Word of God (see **Ephesians 6: 10-17**).

You are now armed with a new level of strength, endurance, and power. You are ready to maximize your destiny forcing the devil to recognize that you are empowered through your union with God (see **Ephesians 6**).

The stand you are taking has new reinforcement power and the ability to override the tactics of the enemy in a more penetrating way. Oh yes, woman of God, you are a powerful missile called to execute the enemy and march forth in new victory!

The final phase in victory involves steadfast prayer. As a praying woman, you are stomping on the head of the enemy. You have the ability to decree the word and cause the heavens to respond immediately. After all, even Jesus divinely interrupted the traditions of the time by allowing himself to be unveiled to a woman before He introduced Himself to the rest of the world at the tomb prior to His resurrection.

Even today, Divine interruptions are still taking place through women. This means that each day a maximized woman wakes up in the morning and decrees the Word of God. Things wake us and shake us. Your prayers are keys that bind and loose. Therefore, you cause things in the earth realm to readjust and get into Divine alignment.

Woman of God, as you decree the Word of God, you can cause dry places to become watered, empty places to become full, and hurt places to become healed. The power of your mouth is a sword that cuts the head of the enemy and causes supernatural breakthrough (see **Proverbs 4:23**)!

You are armed and dangerous and you are ready to pray the fire from the heavenlies to interrupt the plans of the enemy. MAXIMIZE the fullness of your Destiny for the sake of your LEGACY!

YOU ARE GOD'S MAXIMIZED WOMAN: ARMED AND DANGEROUS!!

BIOGRAPHY OF THE AUTHOR

Dr. Lorelle Rich is a graduate of Howard University, where she obtained a Bachelor of Arts degree in Television Broadcasting. She also obtained a Master of Divinity from Vanderbilt University and a Doctorate in Christian Counseling from World Bible College. Dr. Rich was the first woman ordained at Mount Zion Baptist Church in Nashville, TN by Bishop Joseph Warren Walker, III.

Dr. Rich has a heart to motivate the lives of God's women to move forward in their destiny and pursue the heartbeat of God. Dr. Rich is also a Christian Therapist who helps the brokenhearted through the Word of God. She is an etiquette coach for youth and adults to assist in the external wholeness of God's people. Dr. Rich serves as a prophetic, yet humble, mouthpiece for the building of God's Kingdom.

Dr. Rich and her husband, Michael D. Rich, Sr., are Senior Pastors and founders of Royal Life International Church. They have locations in Madison and Smyrna, Tennessee. She is the proud mother of two children, Majesty and Michael Rich Jr.

CONNECT TODAY WITH DR. RICH!!

Dr. Rich has an empowering **Free Teleconference line** each Monday at 6:30 p.m. (CST). She reaches lives all over the world. Please join Dr. Rich **LIVE** so she can empower you by dialing 1-218-548-0943, pass code 64364448#.

Dr. Rich is on Facebook and each Tuesday has a live message on www.cinchcast.com/lsrtalks. You can connect with Dr. Rich throughout the week and allow the impartation of God's anointing to touch your life TODAY!! This information and more can be found on her website at www.lsrtalks.com. Visit her online TODAY!!

If you would like to contact Dr. Lorelle Rich, please email lsrtalks@aol.com or visit her website.

Accept Jesus Christ as your personal Savior Today. He is the only doorway to salvation (see **Romans 10:9-10**). If you have done this, find a church home so that you can continue to grow in your spiritual walk.

A Maximized Woman: Armed and Dangerous
Coming Soon!

Other Books Coming Soon by
Dr. Lorelle Rich

From The Bedroom to the Throneroom

Effective Keys to Supernatural Wealth

10 Destiny Keys
to Being a Successful Woman

Destiny Is Calling You

Bondage Breaker Prayer Strategies

www.ingramcontent.com/pod-product-compliance
Lightning Source LLC
LaVergne TN
LVHW051155080426
835508LV00021B/2641